THE CHINESE
MENU COOKBOOK

by
Constance D. Chang

Doubleday & Company, Inc.

Garden City, New York

1974

ISBN: 0-385-00658-6
Library of Congress Catalogue Card Number 72-144257
Copyright © 1969 by Shufunotomo Co., Ltd.
All Rights Reserved
Printed in Japan

PREFACE

It is not my wish to publish another cookbook consisting of many recipes for various Chinese dishes. There are already scores of Chinese cookbooks on the market; and I have already had several cookbooks published in Tokyo, London, San Francisco and Hawaii. Nor do I find it necessary to introduce Chinese food in general or some special dishes in particular in this book, since Chinese food is so popular today.

In my more than twenty years of experience in establishing and supervising seven restaurants in Japan (four "Peacock Hall" buffets in the Tokyu Hotels in Tokyo, Yokohama, Haneda, and Fukuoka; and three other restaurants called "Madame Chang's Home Kitchen" at Shibuya, Seijo and Nihonbashi in Tokyo), I have observed that most people, whether Japanese or tourists from any part of the world or even Chinese, do not seem to know what dishes to order. They make the mistake of ordering perhaps their favorite dishes but not the best combination for a good meal according to the Chinese standard. Then in 1958 I initiated the first Chinese buffet restaurants in Japan, where a great variety of dishes are served on a special counter with devices to keep the food warm. The customers can come up and select what they want at a nominal cost without having to face the problem of ordering, in other words of making up a menu. The successful result of the buffet restaurants demonstrates that people need to be introduced to the "know-how" of the Chinese menu. It is difficult, indeed, to select the right dishes to produce a balanced meal, but it is essential in Chinese food.

The basic principles of a Chinese menu apply to ordering in a restaurant as well as to cooking in your own kitchen. These are illustrated in this book with recipes grouped into six sets of suggested menus, consisting of five courses each to serve four to six persons. The recipes are simple and easy-to-follow with step-by-step illustrations. All ingredients called for are available at any supermarket and no special kitchen utensils other than a frying pan and a sauce pan, etc., are required.

These recipes are interchangeable from the menus (see chart below) and may be combined to make as many as 150 assorted menus:

A	B	C	D	E	F	......	A	B	C	D	E	F	......
1	1	1	1	1	1	......	A1	B1	C1	A1	D1	F1	......
2	2	2	2	2	2	......	B2	E2	E2	C2	F2	E2	......
3	3	3	3	3	3	......	C3	C3	B3	E3	D3	B3	......
4	4	4	4	4	4	......	D4	F4	F4	B4	A4	A4	......
5	5	5	5	5	5	......	E5	D5	D5	F5	C5	A5	......

and so on.

The simplest Chinese meal consists of one soup and one dish, served with steamed rice, when one is eating alone. A Chinese meal often consists of eight or more than ten courses depending upon the occasion and the number of persons present. During the Ching Dynasty, there was a special banquet called "滿漢全席" (Man-Han Complete Feast) that comprised 100 courses and lasted two to three days. Of course, today it is impossible to serve such an extravagant meal as nobody would have time to waste like this. A regular meal at home consists of four or five dishes. The suggested menus given in this book can be used for a small gathering or for the family.

The Chinese menu emphasizes variety; for instance, varieties in the following:

1) ingredients (i.e., vegetables, pork, beef, seafood, etc.);
2) ways of cooking (i.e., steaming, boiling, sauté (stir frying), stewing, deep-frying, etc.);
3) ways of cutting (i.e., slicing, dicing, shredding, oblique-cutting, cutting in chunks, etc.);
4) flavoring (i.e., salt, garlic, chili, soy sauce, sugar, vinegar, etc.)

A balanced meal of, say, five dishes, must consist of one meat (pork or beef), one vegetable, one seafood (fish or shrimp), soup and dessert. If you want to add one more, then perhaps one dish of chicken. For example, take Menu E on page 42:

	1	2	3	4
E1	Soup (Won Ton)	boiling	minced meat	salt
E2	Vegetable (eggplant)	sauté	slicing lengthwise	garlic
E3	Seafood (shrimp)	stewed	n/a	chili
E4	Chicken	deep-frying	chunks	soy sauce
E5	Dessert (orange)	heating	juice	sugar

Chinese cooking is considered an art; each dish, therefore, should be well prepared to delight the senses. According to the Chinese saying, there are 3 conditions—"色, 香, 味" it should appeal to the eye—color; to the nose—aroma; and to the palate—taste.

For the overseas readers of this book who do not have the opportunity to watch my TV program "Today's Cooking" (Japan National Broadcasting Station, NHK) and who are unable to join one of my cooking classes in Japan, why not try the simple recipes in this book? The results will look the same as those in the color pictures, and will taste delicious too. By using this book as a reference, I am sure that you will be able to plan and cook authentic Chinese menus, as well as order in a Chinese restaurant with confidence.

Constance D. Chang

CONTENTS

Directions

1. Recipes from each menu are interchangeable and may be combined to make an infinite number of assorted menus.

2. Each menu is to be served for 6 persons.

3. Unless otherwise specified, vegetable oil is used for frying, and the dishes are to be served hot.

4. Hints and suggestions on table setting and for hors d'oeuvre and beverages are given on pages 62—64.

MENU A

(6 SERVINGS)

1. Tomato Clam Soup
2. Deep Fried
   Walnuts Chicken
3. Sweet-Sour Pork
4. Cucumber Salad
5. Egg Fried Rice

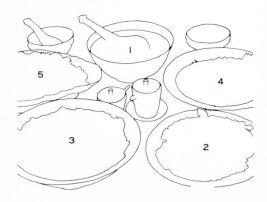

蕃茄蛤肉湯
TOMATO CLAM SOUP

Ingredients:

3 dozen small-sized clams, unshucked
3 tomatoes (about 1½ lb.)
5 cups chicken stock
1 tablespoon scallion, diced diagonally

3 tablespoons oil
½ teaspoon pepper
1½ teaspoons salt
1½ tablespoons cornstarch mixed in 3
    tablespoons water
salad or sesame oil

Method:

1. Boil clams in 2½ cups of water until bivalves open, pick out meat and wash away sand.
2. Blanch tomatoes for half a minute, peel off skin and cut into 6 or 8 wedges.
3. Heat oil and fry tomato pieces until soft. Strain, using a piece of clean gauze or a sieve, and discard pulp. To tomato, add chicken stock, clams, pepper and salt. Cook for 2 minutes. Add scallion and cornstarch mixture. Stir until boiling and sprinkle a dash of salad or sesame oil on surface. Serve in a warmed soup bowl.

OVER MEDIUM HEAT

5

炸核桃鷄片

DEEP FRIED WALNUTS CHICKEN

Ingredients:

½ lb. chicken breasts
2 egg whites
4 tablespoons cornstarch
2 cups walnuts, chopped
canned pineapple ⎫
maraschino cherry ⎬ for garnish
green pepper ⎭

(a) ⎧ 1½ teaspoons salt
⎨ pepper
⎩ 2 teaspoons sherry
4 cups oil for frying

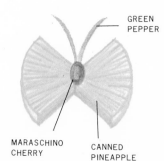

GREEN
PEPPER

MARASCHINO
CHERRY

CANNED
PINEAPPLE

I

2-3

3

4

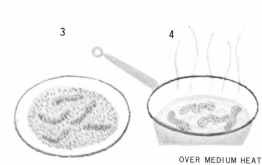

OVER MEDIUM HEAT

Method:

1. Cut chicken breasts into bite size and mix with (a).
2. Beat egg white lightly, add cornstarch and mix well.
3. Dip chicken into egg-white mixture and coat with walnuts.
4. Heat oil to 375° F. Drop walnut-coated chicken, one by one, into pan and deep fry until light brown. Remove from oil and drain. Place on a serving plate and garnish with pineapple, cherry and green pepper arranged like a butterfly (see photo).

咕 咾 肉
SWEET-SOUR PORK

Ingredients:

1 lb. lean boneless pork

(a) { 1 teaspoon sherry
½ teaspoon salt
¼ teaspoon pepper

(b) { 1 egg
1 tablespoon flour
1 tablespoon cornstarch

5 cups oil for frying
⅓ of a carrot, peeled and parboiled, cut in bite size
3 dried mushrooms, soaked and quartered
3 cups onion, cut in bite size
⅔ cup cucumber, cut in bite size
1 clove garlic, peeled and sliced

(c) { 4 tablespoons tomato ketchup
1 teaspoon soy sauce
4 tablespoons vinegar
4 tablespoons sugar
¾ cup water
1½ tablespoons cornstarch

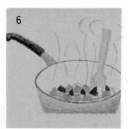

Method:

1. Cut meat into bite size.
2. Sprinkle sherry, salt and pepper of (a) on all sides.
3. Mix (b) in a bowl and dip pork into it. Heat frying oil to 375° F. Fry pork until light brown, one by one. Remove from oil and drain.
4. Sauté vegetables all at once in same pan for 1 minute. Remove from pan and drain.
5. Mix (c) well together. Heat 5 tablespoons oil in another pan, add (c) mixture and cook until thick.
6. Return pork and vegetables into sauce and mix well.

OVER MEDIUM HEAT

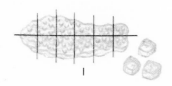

凉拍黄瓜

CUCUMBER SALAD

Ingredients:

6 radishes
½ of a cucumber (about ¾ lb.)
⅓ cup carrot, shredded

1 teaspoon salt
1 tablespoon salad oil
2 teaspoons sugar
3 tablespoons vinegar
3 tablespoons soy sauce
½ teaspoon MSG (monosodium glutamate)

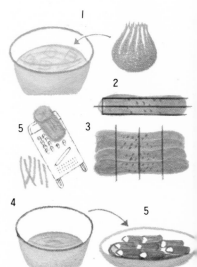

Method:

1. Prepare radish flowers as illustrated. Soak in ice water with ½ teaspoon salt for 20 minutes.
2. Cut cucumber and remove seeds. Pound lightly with flat of heavy knife or cleaver.
3. Cut cucumber into 1 or 2 inch lengths.
4. Mix ½ teaspoon salt, salad oil, sugar, vinegar, soy sauce and MSG well.
5. Pour (4) over cucumber. Garnish with radish and carrot.

蛋 炒 飯

EGG
FRIED
RICE

Ingredients:

7 eggs
4 cups cold cooked white rice (see page 21)
½ cup ham, chopped
3 tablespoons green peas
⅓ cup scallion, shredded
3 tablespoons oil
¾ teaspoon salt
¼ teaspoon MSG (monosodium glutamate)

Method:

1. Beat eggs in a bowl, adding a pinch of salt and MSG.
2. Heat oil, add eggs and cook for 1 minute over medium heat.
3. Add rice and fry well, mixing with eggs.
4. Add ham, green peas, scallion, salt and MSG, mixing well until heated through.

MENU B

(6 SERVINGS)

1. Vegetable Soup
2. Beef with Snow Peas
3. Deep Fried Pork
4. Fresh Ginger Oyster
5. Boiled Rice

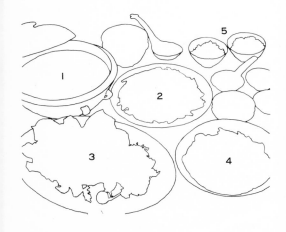

素菜湯
VEGETABLE SOUP

Ingredients:

1 tomato (about 8 oz.)
6 cups chicken stock
3 cups cabbage, shredded
½ cup carrot, julienne
1 cup onion, thinly sliced
1 cup celery, julienne

3 tablespoons oil
1 tablespoon salt
¼ teaspoon pepper
¼ teaspoon MSG (monosodium glutamate)
1 teaspoon sesame or salad oil
½ teaspoon Tabasco (optional)

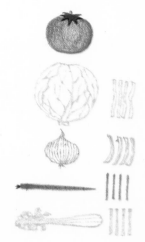

Method:

1. Blanch tomato for half a minute and slip off skin.   Remove seeds and cut into small pieces.
2. In boiling chicken stock add cabbage, carrot, onion and celery and bring to boil again.   Reduce heat and cook until tender.
3. Sauté tomato in 3 tablespoons oil.   Add to soup with salt, pepper and MSG. Cook for another 3 or 4 minutes and add sesame oil and Tabasco.

15

雪豆牛肉

BEEF WITH SNOW PEAS

Ingredients:

12 oz. beef fillet

(a)
- ⅓ teaspoon baking soda
- ¾ teaspoon sugar
- ½ teaspoon salt
- 1½ teaspoons cornstarch
- 1½ tablespoons soy sauce
- 2 tablespoons water

1½ cups snow peas, strung
1 teaspoon fresh ginger or ¼ teaspoon ginger powder
4-inch long scallion
4 cups oil for frying

(b)
- 1 teaspoon cornstarch
- 1 tablespoon water
- 1 tablespoon sesame or salad oil

½ teaspoon salt

Method:

1. Cut beef in bite-size slices, marinate in (a) for 30 minutes, then add 2 tablespoons oil and mix well.
2. Heat frying oil and deep fry beef for 1 minute. Drain. Pound fresh ginger and scallion lightly.
3. Leave 2 tablespoons oil in pan, fry ginger and scallion and add (b) mixture. Cook until thick. Remove ginger and scallion. Stir in beef and mix well for 1 minute. Remove to hot serving plate.
4. Heat 2 tablespoons oil, add ½ teaspoon salt and cook snow peas for 2 minutes. Arrange on serving plate as garnish.

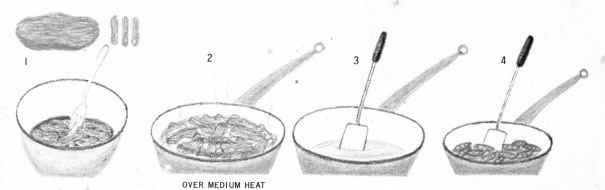

1   2   3   4

OVER MEDIUM HEAT

17

油 炸 肉
DEEP FRIED PORK

Ingredients:

1¼ lb. pork brisket or pork chop
4-inch long scallion
1½ tablespoons sherry
4 tablespoons soy sauce
¼ teaspoon ginger powder
4 cups oil for frying
1 tablespoon sugar
3 potatoes (about 1¼ lb.)
leaf lettuce

370°F

Method:

1. Cut pork into 1-inch by 2-inch pieces. With flat of knife pound scalion lightly. Marinate pork in sherry, soy sauce, ginger powder and scallion for 30 minutes.
2. Heat oil and deep fry pork until brown. Remove from oil and drain.
3. Heat marinade. Add sugar, cook for a few seconds, return fried pork to sauce and stir well. Remove to plate.
4. Peel potatoes and cut into finger size strips. Soak in cold water and drain. Deep fry in oil until light brown.
5. Remove to serving plate and garnish with leaf lettuce.

19

薑葱生蠔

FRESH GINGER OYSTER

Ingredients:
    30 oysters, shucked
    8-inch long scallion, cut in ½-inch lengths
    1 tablespoon fresh ginger, sliced
    2 cloves garlic, sliced

    5 tablespoons oil
    4 tablespoons sherry
    4 tablespoons soy sauce
    ⅓ teaspoon salt
    ½ tablespoon sugar

Method:
1. In boiling water add oysters and cook for 30 seconds. Wash and drain well.
2. Heat oil. Add scallion, ginger and garlic and fry for a few seconds. Add oyster, sherry, soy sauce, salt and sugar all at once. Stir quickly over high heat.

MENU B-5

BOILED RICE

Ingredients:
    3 cups rice
    3½ cups water

Method:
1. Wash rice in large bowl with cold water by rubbing gently between thumb and fingers. Drain and repeat this procedure 5 or 6 times until water is clear. Drain well and set aside for 30 minutes.
2. Put drained rice and water in covered pan and cook over high heat. When it comes to boil, reduce the heat to low and cook for 10 minutes more. Turn flame on high again and remove from heat.
3. Let stand, covered, for about 10 minutes before serving.

MENU C

(6 SERVINGS)

1. Chicken Noodle Soup
2. Vegetable Toast
3. Creamed Chinese Cabbage
4. Shredded Beef with
   Green Pepper & Onion
5. Steamed Chinese Cake

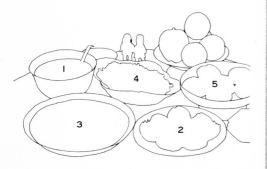

鷄湯麵

CHICKEN NOODLE SOUP

Ingredients:

2 oz. vermicelli or noodle

2½ oz. chicken breasts

12 snow peas

7 cups chicken stock

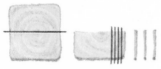

⅓ cup ham, cut into strips

¼ cup dried mushroom, soaked and shredded

⅓ cup canned bamboo shoots, cut into strips

¼ cup carrot, cut into strips

1 tablespoon salt
pepper
MSG (monosodium glutamate)

Method:
1. Drop vermicelli into boiling water and boil for 5 minutes. Drain, rinse and drain again. Set aside.
2. Slice chicken meat and snow peas into thin strips.
3. Bring chicken stock to boiling point. Add chicken meat, ham, snow peas, mushroom, bamboo shoots and carrot. Cook for 2 minutes. Add seasonings and cooked vermicelli and boil for 1 minute over medium heat.

素 炸吐司
VEGETABLE TOAST

Ingredients:

2 potatoes (about 1 lb.)
3 tablespoons carrot, grated
1 egg white
6 slices bread (sandwich thickness)
4 tablespoons ham, chopped
3 tablespoons parsley, minced
1 teaspoon black or white sesame seeds

1½ tablespoons salt
MSG (monosodium glutamate)
1½ tablespoons cornstarch
4 cups oil for frying
2 green peppers for garnish
tomato ketchup
French mustard

OVER MEDIUM HEAT

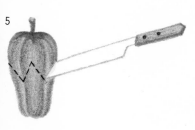

Method:

1. Peel and boil potato, drain and mash.
2. Mix carrot with mashed potato, add salt, MSG, beaten egg white and cornstarch and mix well.
3. Cut bread into 2 inch rounds. Spread mixture on each round. Sprinkle with ham, parsley and sesame seeds, pressing down lightly to make garnish adhere.
4. Heat oil and deep fry bread, first potato side down, then turn over. Fry until turn golden brown. Remove to plate.
5. Cut tops off green peppers to make 2 small dishes (see photo) to hold tomato ketchup and French mustard.

奶油白菜

CREAMED CHINESE CABBAGE

Ingredients:

1 small-sized Chinese cabbage (about 2 lb.)
1 teaspoon salt

(a) {
2 cups milk
1½ tablespoons cornstarch
¾ teaspoon salt
MSG (monosodium glutamate)
}

6 tablespoons oil
1 hard-cooked egg yolk, minced
parsley, minced
1 teaspoon paprika

Method:

1. Parboil Chinese cabbage in water with 1 teaspoon salt until tender and drain.   Then cut it into 3 or 4 inches lengths.
2. Mix (a) well together, and set aside.
3. Heat oil, add cabbage and sauté for 2 minutes.   Add milk mixture and stir well until thicken.   Remove to warmed plate and sprinkle with egg yolk, parsley and paprika.

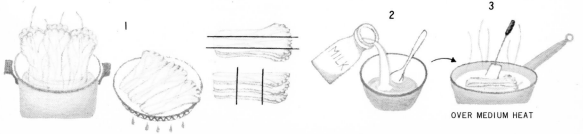

OVER MEDIUM HEAT

青椒牛肉絲

SHREDDED BEEF WITH GREEN PEPPER AND ONION

Ingredients:

14 oz. beef rump steak, shredded

(a)
- 2 teaspoons oil
- 1 tablespoon sherry
- 1 teaspoon cornstarch
- ¼ teaspoon baking soda
- 1 tablespoon soy sauce
- ½ teaspoon sugar

6 tablespoons oil
¾ teaspoon salt
2 cups onion, shredded
1 cup green pepper, shredded
pepper

Method:

1. Sprinkle beef with (a). Set aside for 30 minutes.
2. Heat 3 tablespoons oil in pan and add ¾ teaspoon salt. Stir in onions and fry for 2 minutes. Add green peppers; fry for 2 minutes. Remove from pan.
3. Heat 3 more tablespoons oil in same pan. Add beef. Stir until colour changes. Add a pinch of pepper and vegetables. Mix well for 1 minute.

OVER MEDIUM HEAT

30

清蒸蛋糕

STEAMED CHINESE CAKE

Ingredients:

6 eggs
6 tablespoons sugar
6 tablespoons flour
almond extract
2 tablespoons raisins
6 each candied red and green
cherries or other candied fruit
lard or shortening

Method:

1. Beat egg and sugar hard with wire whisk.
2. Add flour and a few drops of almond extract and mix well, but gently.
3. Chop candied fruit. Grease 6 pyrex cups with lard or shortening. Sprinkle with fruit on bottom of cups. Pour batter over this.
4. Steam for 20 minutes. Remove gently and set on warmed plate.

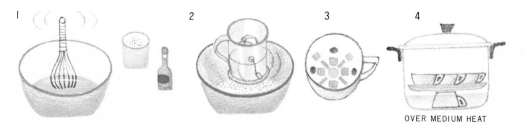

OVER MEDIUM HEAT

MENU D
(6 SERVINGS)

1. Sour & Hot Soup
2. Braised Pork
   with Chestnuts
3. Egg Sandwich Chinese
4. Sweet & Sour Prawns
5. Glazed Apples

酸辣湯

SOUR AND HOT SOUP

Ingredients:

    2 oz. boneless pork, shredded
    5 cups chicken stock
    ½ cup carrot, parboiled and shredded
    ½ cup dried Chinese mushrooms, soaked
    with warm water and shredded
    ⅓ cup canned bamboo shoots, shredded
    ½ cup ham, shredded
    3 eggs, beaten

    6 teaspoons cornstarch
    1½ teaspoons salt
    2 tablespoons soy sauce
    ½ teaspoon pepper
    2 tablespoons vinegar
    4½ tablespoons water
    ¼ teaspoon MSG (monosodium glutamate)

Method:

1. Dredge pork with pinch of salt and pepper
    and 1 teaspoon cornstarch.
2. Bring chicken stock to boil.   Add salt, pork,
    carrot, mushroom, bamboo shoots and ham,
    cooking for 2 minutes.   Add mixture of soy
    sauce, pepper, vinegar, cornstarch, water
    and MSG.   Stir for a few seconds until soup
    thickens.
3. Slowly pour in beaten eggs in a fine thread,
    stirring gently.   Add pepper for taste.*

*   If you prefer hot seasoning, you may add a
    few drops of Tabasco.

OVER MEDIUM HEAT

栗子紅燒肉

BRAISED PORK WITH CHESTNUTS

OVER MEDIUM HEAT

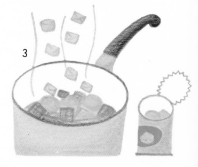

Ingredients:

2 lb. pork shoulder or fresh ham
¼ of a scallion, thinly sliced on di-
agonal
1 teaspoon fresh ginger, chopped,
or ¼ teaspoon ginger powder
18 canned or fresh* chestnuts

6 tablespoons oil
2 tablespoons sherry
6 tablespoons soy sauce
1½ cups water
3 tablespoons rock candy
or crystalized sugar

Method:

1. Cut pork into 1 inch cubes.
2. Heat 6 tablespoons oil.   Add scallion, ginger and pork cubes.
   Stir until pork changes colour.   Add sherry, soy sauce and
   water; bring to boil.   Cover pan and reduce heat to low.
   Simmer for 20 minutes.
3. Add canned chestnuts and rock candy.   Cook for another 20
   minutes.
* If fresh chestnuts are used, boil and peel off shells and inner
   brown membranes, add rock candy and cook for 30 minutes.

荷 包 蛋

EGG
SANDWICH
CHINESE

Ingredients:

6 eggs
lettuce leaves
6 butter rolls

3 teaspoons oil
2 tablespoons soy sauce
1 teaspoon sugar
1 tablespoon water

Method:

1. Break one egg into small bowl.
2. Heat ½ teaspoon oil and fry each egg separately. When egg has set, fold over in half-moon shape. Remove to plate.
3. Add soy sauce, sugar, water to same pan, bring to boil, add eggs and cook for 1½ minutes.
4. Put fried egg and lettuce leaf between split rolls (see photo).

OVER MEDIUM HEAT

烹 大 蝦

SWEET AND SOUR PRAWNS

Ingredients:

12 prawns
1 cucumber, sliced

salt
pepper
1 teaspoon cornstarch
4 cups oil

(a) {
3 tablespoons soy sauce
3 tablespoons vinegar
1½ tablespoons sherry
1½ tablespoons sugar
⅓ teaspoon salt
3 teaspoons cornstarch
¼ teaspoon MSG (monosodium glutamate)
}

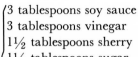

Method:

1. Wash prawns and remove shell except at tail. Remove black veins and slice along back, without cutting through, as shown in illustration. Sprinkle a dash of salt and pepper and coat with cornstarch.
2. Heat frying oil to 375° F. Add prawns, fry for 1 minute, remove from oil and drain.
3. Mix seasonings (a) in a bowl.
4. Heat 3 tablespoons oil in pan, cook (a) mixture until thick. Place prawns into mixture and mix well. Garnish with cucumber.

拔絲蘋菓
GLAZED APPLES

How to make syrup:

Ingredients:

   3 medium-sized apples (about 12 oz.)
   2 egg whites
   4 tablespoons all-purpose flour
   2 teaspoons cornstarch
   1 teaspoon black or white sesame seeds

   salt
   4 cups oil for frying
   2 tablespoons water
   1⅓ cups sugar

Method:

1. Cut apple into 8 wedges; peel and core. Place in water with salt added.
2. Beat egg white and mix with flour and cornstarch until smooth.
3. Drain apples and coat with batter.
4. Heat oil to 375° F. Deep fry apples until light amber, remove from oil and drain.
5. Bring water and sugar to boil over high heat, stirring, only until sugar dissolves. Add 1 tablespoon oil, stir constantly until syrup instantly forms hard mass in iced water. Put fried apples and black or white sesame seeds into syrup.*
6. Remove well-coated glazed apples to lightly greased serving plate. Dip each piece quickly into bowl of ice water before eating.

  * Syrup should form threads as you remove the apples (see photo).

MENU E

(6 SERVINGS)

1. Won Ton Soup
2. Eggplant with Meat & Garlic
3. Shrimp in Hot Sauce
4. Deep Fried Chicken
5. Hot Orange Juice

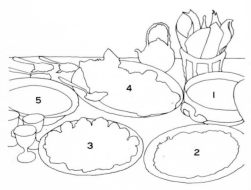

餛飩湯
WON TON SOUP

Ingredients:

For won ton skin:
1 egg
6 tablespoons water
3 cups flour

For filling:
1 cup spinach leaves, boiled and
chopped
¾ cup minced pork
½ teaspoon salt
½ teaspoon sugar
¼ teaspoon pepper
¼ teaspoon MSG (monosodium
glutamate)
2 teaspoons sherry

6 cups chicken stock
12 snow peas, boiled
egg sheet*, cut into strips
1 tablespoon scallion, shredded
diagonally (optional)

Method:

To make won ton skin:
1. In bowl beat egg and mix with water. Add
flour and mix well.
2. Knead for about 1 minute into stiff dough.
Cover with damp cloth and set aside for about
30 minutes.
3. Roll out dough about 1/16 inch thick. Cut out
20 squares, 3 inches by 3 inches, for won ton
skins.

To make won ton:
1. Mix spinach, pork, salt, sugar, pepper, MSG and
sherry well.
2. Place ½ teaspoon of meat mixture in centre of
each skin. Bring opposite corners together in
fold. Seal by dotting bottom edge with water
and pinching together firmly. Fold other two
corners toward each other. See illustration.
3. Cook won ton in boiling water for 2 minutes and
remove to 6 individual bowls.
4. Bring chicken stock to boil, add a pinch of salt
and pepper and pour broth over won ton.
5. Garnish with snow peas, egg sheet and scallion
and serve immediately.

* To make egg sheet:
1. Beat one egg with a pinch of salt, sherry and MSG.
2. Heat 1 teaspoon oil in frying pan over medium heat, cooking pan evenly.
3. Pour in egg rotating quickly to cover bottom of pan.
4. Cook until lightly browned. Remove to cutting board and cut into strips.

45

魚香茄子

EGGPLANT WITH MEAT AND GARLIC

Ingredients:

2 large-sized eggplants
5 oz. ground pork
3 tablespoons Chinese mushroom, soaked and chopped
2 teaspoons garlic, minced

4 cups oil for frying
2½ tablespoons soy sauce
1½ tablespoons sherry
½ teaspoon cornstarch
pepper
1 teaspoon salt
1 teaspoon sugar
1 teaspoon salad or sesame oil

Method:

1. Remove stems from eggplants. Cut each into 12 lengthwise pieces and cut gashes in each piece (as shown).
2. In oil heated to 375° F., deep fry eggplant for 2 minutes.
3. Combine soy sauce, sherry and cornstarch and mix with ground pork, mushroom and garlic.
4. Heat 3 tablespoons oil in pan, sauté pork mixture for 2 minutes. Add fried eggplant and mix well. Add a dash of pepper, salt and sugar and stir well. Quickly stir in salad or sesame oil.

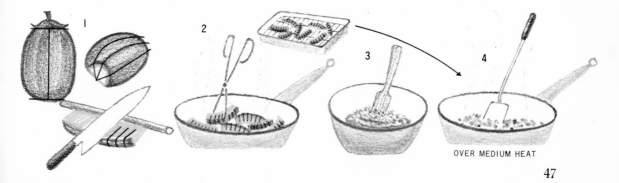

OVER MEDIUM HEAT

干燒蝦仁

SHRIMP IN HOT SAUCE

Ingredients:

2½ cups (1 lb.) shelled shrimps
1½ tablespoons fresh ginger, minced, or
½ teaspoon ginger powder
1 tablespoon garlic, minced
6 tablespoons scallion, sliced
broccoli

(a) { 1 tablespoon sherry
½ egg white
1 teaspoon cornstarch }

2 cups oil for frying

(b) { 2 teaspoons Tabasco
4½ tablespoons tomato ketchup
1 tablespoon soy sauce
1 tablespoon sugar
1½ teaspoons vinegar
½ teaspoon salt }

⅓ cup chicken stock or water
2 tablespoons cornstarch combined with 3 or
    4 tablespoons water

Method:

1. Remove black vein from shrimps, wash in salted water and drain. Mix with (a).
2. Divide clusters of flower buds of broccoli and boil in salted water. Arrange on serving plate as garnish.
3. In oil heated to 350°F·, sauté shrimps, stirring briskly. Do not overcook. Remove from oil and drain.
4. In 6 tablespoons heated oil sauté ginger, garlic and scallion for 1 minute. Add (b) and shrimps. Pour in chicken stock or water, cook for 2 minutes, stirring constantly. Thicken with cornstarch. Remove to serving plate.

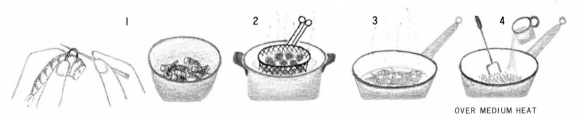

OVER MEDIUM HEAT

炸 子 鶏
DEEP FRIED CHICKEN

Ingredients:
12 chicken legs
½ cup scallion, shredded

(a) {
4 tablespoons soy sauce
2 tablespoons sherry
¼ teaspoon pepper
}
½ cup cornstarch
4 cups frying oil

OVER MEDIUM HEAT

Method:
1. Marinate chicken legs in (a) for 30 minutes.
2. Coat each chicken leg with cornstarch. In oil heated to 375° F., fry chicken legs until golden brown and drain.
3. Drain pan, put in scallions and fried chicken legs, stirring over heat for 1 minute so scallions stick to chicken. If desired, garnish plate with flower made from giant radish, as shown in photo.

橙 子 羹

HOT ORANGE JUICE

Ingredients:
 4 cups water
 1¹/₂ cups sugar
 3 oranges, squeezed
 3 oranges, sectioned
 3 tablespoons cornstarch combined with 3 tablespoons water
 3 maraschino cherries
 angelica, sliced

Method:
1. Combine water and sugar in saucepan; bring to boil over high heat. Add orange juice and sections, stirring until sugar is dissolved. Add cornstarch mixture, stirring constantly until thickened. Pour into serving bowl garnished with sliced cherries and angelica as shown in photo.

51

MENU F

(6 SERVINGS)

1. Tomato Egg Soup
2. Sweet & Sour Cabbage
3. Braised Duck in Wine
4. Shrimp Chow-Mein
5. Almond Jelly

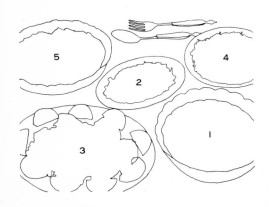

蕃茄蛋花湯

TOMATO
EGG
SOUP

Ingredients:

- 1 tomato
- 5 cups chicken stock
- 1 egg, beaten
- a few spinach sprays

- 1½ teaspoons salt
- ¼ teaspoon MSG (monosodium glutamate)
- 1 teaspoon salad or sesame oil

Method:

1. Cut tomato into thin wedges, removing seeds.
2. Bring tomato and chicken stock to boil. Add salt and MSG.
3. Pour beaten egg in fine thread and bring to boil.
   Add spinach sprays and again bring to boil. Remove from heat and sprinkle with salad oil.

糖醋卷心菜

SWEET AND SOUR CABBAGE

Ingredients:

14 cups cabbage, shredded
$1\frac{1}{2}$ cups green pepper, shredded
$\frac{1}{2}$ cup fresh red pepper or pimento, shredded

6 tablespoons oil
$1\frac{1}{2}$ teaspoons salt
$4\frac{1}{2}$ tablespoons vinegar
$4\frac{1}{2}$ tablespoons sugar
$\frac{1}{4}$ teaspoon MSG (monosodium glutamate)

OVER MEDIUM HEAT

Method:

1. Heat 3 tablespoons oil in pan, add salt first, then peppers. Stir for 1 minute and remove to plate.
2. Heat 3 tablespoons oil in same pan, add cabbage, cook for 2 minutes. Add peppers and mix well.
3. Mix together vinegar, sugar and MSG, and add to pan; cook, tossing well for 2 or 3 minutes. Serve hot or cold.

酒燜鴨

BRAISED DUCK IN WINE

Ingredients:

1 duck (about 4½ lb.), cut in serving pieces
¼ of a leek
1 orange

1 cup dry sherry
⅓ cup water
6 tablespoons soy sauce
2 tablespoons rock candy or crystalized sugar

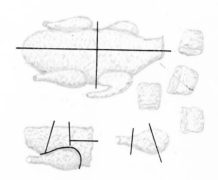

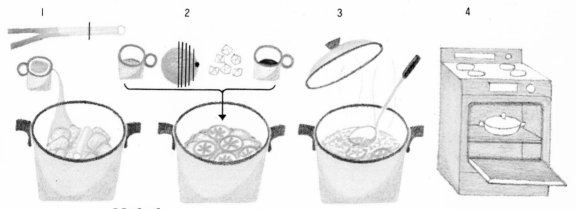

Method:

1. Put duck into Dutch oven with leek and sherry and bring to boil.
2. Slice orange.   Add half of it to pan.   Add water, soy sauce and rock candy.
3. Cover and reduce heat to low and cook for 20 minutes.
4. Transfer to 375° F. oven, braise for 1 hour.   Remove to hot dish.   Garnish with orange slices.

蝦仁炒麵
SHRIMP CHOW-MEIN

Ingredients:

¾ lb. thin spaghetti (Chinese noodles if available)
5 oz. shelled shrimp (frozen)
2½ cups spinach

1⅔ teaspoons salt
pepper
5 teaspoons sherry
4½ tablespoons oil
MSG (monosodium glutamate)

Method:

1. Cook spaghetti in boiling water and drain.
2. Wash shrimp first in 2 cups of water with 1 teaspoon salt added, then rinse with cold water and drain. Sprinkle with a dash of pepper and 2 teaspoons sherry.
3. Cut spinach into 2 or 3 inches lengths. Wash and drain.
4. Heat 1½ tablespoons oil in pan, sauté shrimp, add ⅓ teaspoon salt, stir for 1 minute over high heat and remove from pan.
5. Heat 1½ tablespoons oil in same pan, add ⅓ teaspoon salt first, then spinach. Toss quickly for half a minute over high heat and remove from pan.
6. Heat 1½ tablespoons oil in same pan. Add spaghetti, shrimp, spinach and 3 teaspoons sherry and stir well. Add pinch of salt and MSG.

杏仁豆腐

ALMOND JELLY

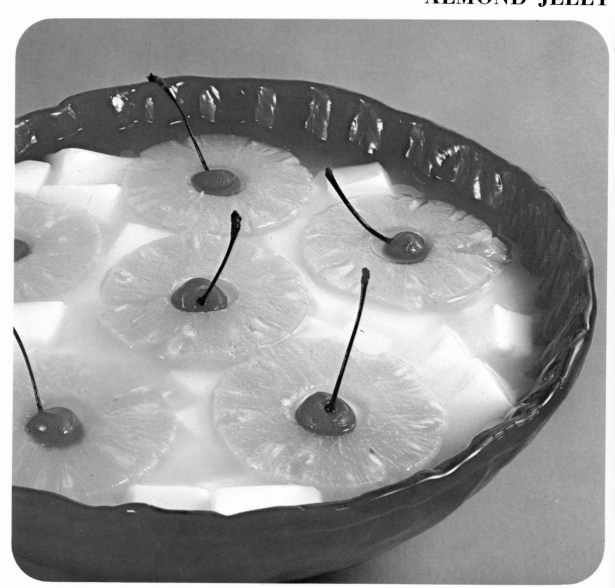

Ingredients:

2 packages unflavoured gelatin (about 2 tablespoons)
1 cup plus 2 tablespoons water
1 cup milk
¾ cup sugar

almond extract
1 cup sugar ⎫
4 cups water ⎭ for syrup
6 slices pineapple
6 cherries

Method:

1. Sprinkle gelatin on 2 tablespoons water to soften.
2. Bring 1 cup of water to boil.   Add gelatin and stir until dissolved.
3. Stir in milk, sugar and almond extract.
4. Pour mixture into flat pan.   Cool in refrigerator.
5. Bring sugar and water to boil to make syrup.   When cool, chill in refrigerator.
6. Cut almond jelly into diamond shapes and pour syrup over it.   Pour into serving bowl and garnish with pineapple and cherry as shown in photograph.

61

NOTES ON CHINESE COOKING

Chinese method of serving and hospitality

A large serving dish each course is placed in the center of the table. Everyone helps himself using his own chopsticks or serving spoon to bring food from the serving dish to his own plate. This very informal way of serving makes for a hospitable atmosphere for the guests.

Table setting for a Chinese meal

The table setting is shown in the picture. A medium-sized plate for individual servings of food, a soup bowl or tea cup for soup, and chopsticks are set at each place. A bread plate may be used as a second dish for small portions of foods or for discarding chicken bones or shrimp shells. A small dish is needed for soy sauce and seasonings. Serving spoons may be required. Forks are optional and knives unnecessary since everything is cut into bite size. The napkin is placed on the plate. Salt, pepper, soy sauce and mustard are placed on the table ready to use.

SOUP BOWL OR TEA CUP

BREAD PLATE

NAPKIN

SMALL DISH

MEDIUM-SIZED PLATE

How to use chopsticks

(1) Tuck one chopstick under thumb and hold firmly.

(2) Add second chopstick and hold it as you would a pencil.

(3) Hold first chopstick in original position, move the second one up and down. Now you can pick up anything.

Menu (hors d'oeuvres)

A formal Chinese dinner generally begins with a cold appetizer, followed by several hot dishes, including the soup and the sweet dish. When entertaining guests at home "one soup and four dishes" is the basic Chinese menu, but if this is not enough cold appetizers may be placed first in the center of the table as an additional dish. (See illustration.)

Foods used as hors d'oeuvres should be selected for their quality of retaining taste and color for several hours.

In China very special seafoods, meats and vegetables are served as hors d'oeuvres; however, the various items shown in the picture such as ham, boiled eggs, canned asparagus, tomatoes, red cabbage, cucumber, stuffed olives and lettuce are all very easy to obtain. Arrange these to represent flowers in a basket. In addition canned plain abalone, pickles and sausage may be served, arranged attractively according to your taste.

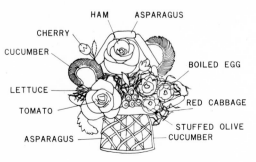

HAM   ASPARAGUS
CHERRY
CUCUMBER
                    BOILED EGG
LETTUCE
                    RED CABBAGE
TOMATO
                    STUFFED OLIVE
ASPARAGUS   CUCUMBER

Beverages

Of course, Chinese wine goes well with Chinese food. *Shoahsing*, a typical wine, is usually served hot, but nice to drink cold, too.

Besides *Mou-tai Chiew*, Japanese wine, beer or Western wine may be served. Green tea or oolong tea is usually served to those who do not care for wine. Jasmine tea is a favorite of some people.

Utensils used for Chinese cooking

The shallow, round-bottomed Chinese frying pan is remarkably handy as it is said all Chinese dishes may be cooked with this one pan.

Of course, the frying pan and sauce pan can be used as substitute, but those who have a keen interest in Chinese cooking would do well to get a Chinese wok. Do not select a stainless steel wok. Although it looks attractive, it tends to scorch and cause foods to stick.

The Chinese pan which is made of iron is the best. A specially shaped turner (see picture) for stirring and mixing completes the set. In addition, there is the basket for steaming and a special flat heavy kitchen knife, but these two are unnecessary for preparing the recipes in this book.

WOK

KITCHEN KNIFE

BASKET FOR STEAMING

About the author:

Madame Constance D. Chang is an authority on Chinese cooking, known for her delicious Chinese food and her recipes for these tasty dishes.

At present, Mrs. Chang has under her direct supervision seven Chinese restaurants in Japan. Peacock Hall is the name given to the four located in the Tokyo, Haneda, Yokohama and Hakata Tokyu Hotels. The other three are called "Madame Chang's Home Kitchen." These serve Chinese snacks and tea and her original Chinese home-style dishes.

Mrs. Chang has the enviable distinction of having initiated the first Chinese buffet restaurants in the world. Only Chinese foods and dishes are served—all you can eat—at a nominal cost.

This intrepid lady has appeared on television cooking programs for more than ten years and has established Chinese cooking schools (three in Tokyo). She has written many books on Chinese cooking. Her cookbooks are illustrated with original drawings, in color, of her dishes which are easy to make and delicious to taste. These attractive cookbooks are a natural outgrowth of the artistry of Mrs. Chang who in her own right is recognized for her Chinese paintings and calligraphy.